ANIMAL WATCH

A Visual Introduction to

BEARS

Facts On File, Inc.
11 Penn Plaza
New York NY 10001

Library of Congress Cataloging-in-Publication Data
Stonehouse, Bernard.
Bears : a visual introduction to bears/Bernard Stonehouse;
illustrated by Martin Camm.
p. cm. – (Animal watch)
Includes index.
Summary: An overview of bears throughout the world
placing each species in its natural environment.
ISBN 0-8160-3923-2 (alk. paper)
1. Bears - Juvenile literature. [1. Bears.] I. Camm, Martin,
ill. II. Title. III. Series: Stonehouse, Bernard. Animal Watch.
QL737.C27S7292 1998
599.78-dc21   98-25083

Facts On File books are available at special discounts when
purchased in bulk quantities for businesses, associations,
institutions or sales promotions. Please call our Special Sales
Department in New York at (212) 967-8800 or (800) 322-8755.

You can find Facts On File on the World Wide Web at
http://www.factsonfile.com

Illustration previous page: Polar bear mother with cubs.

ANIMAL WATCH

A Visual Introduction to

BEARS

Bernard Stonehouse

Illustrated by Martin Camm

Checkmark Books™

An imprint of Facts On File, Inc.

PICTURE CREDITS

BBC Natural History Unit Picture Library
Pages 14-15 lc, rb; 17 rc; 19rc; 35 rc

Frank Lane Picture Agency
Pages 9 rt; 12-13 cb; 18-19 ct, rb; 20 lb; 23 rc; 27 rc; 28-29 ct; 31 rt, rb;
33 rc, rt; 34-35 ct; 36-37 cc; 41 rc; 42-43 all

Minden Pictures/Robert Harding
Pages 22-23 ct

Natural History Photographic Agency
Pages 13 rt, rc; 16-17 rt; 18 lb; 23 rb; 27 rt

Oxford Scientific Films
Pages 8 lb; 17 cb; 30-31 ct; 39 cc

Topham Picturepoint
Pages 21 rt; 22-23 lc, rc

Woodfall Wild Images
Pages 9 rt; 20-21 ct; 24-25 lc, cc; 27 cb; 32-33 ct, rb

WorldSat
All satellite mapping

World Wide Fund for Nature
WWF logo, page 41

Additional artwork:
Susanna Addario, pages 19 tr; 35 tr; 37 c, rt; 39 rt
Claudia Saraceni, pages10 b; 11 br; tr, 37 c

l=left, r=right, c=center, t=top, b=below

Art and editorial direction by **Peter Sackett**

Edited by **Norman Barrett**

Designed by **Paul Richards, Designers & Partners**

Picture research by **Lis Sackett**

Color separation by **Job Color, Italy**

Printed by **Casterman, Belgium**

CONTENTS

FAMILY RELATIONS

Bears are mammals – warm-blooded animals that feed their young on milk. They belong to the order (major group) of mammals called Carnivora, which means "meat-eaters." The ten kinds of living bears, together with many other kinds known only as fossils, make up the family Ursidae.

Other members of the Carnivora include raccoons (family Procyonidae), otters, weasels, skunks and badgers (Mustelidae), dogs, foxes, wolves and jackals (Canidae), mongooses and civets (Viverridae), hyenas (Hyaenidae) and lions, tigers and other cats (Felidae). So bears are related to all these other meat-eating animals, though sufficiently different to make up a family of their own.

RACCOON

BEAR

OTTER

WOLF

MONGOOSE

HYENA

TIGER

Alaskan grizzly bear

THE BEARS AND THEIR RELATIONS

Heavyweight cousins of dogs, wolves and lions, bears are quiet, solitary animals of forests and heathlands.

LARGE, LUMBERING, HEAVILY BUILT animals, bears have dense fur, long noses, dog-like faces, round ears and short stumpy legs, with sloping hindquarters and a very short tail that seldom shows at all. Their feet are broad and flat, with long, forward-pointing claws. In all species, males are usually larger and heavier than females.

Like their closest relations – dogs, wolves, hyenas and other members of the order Carnivora – bears have digestive systems that are specialized for eating meat, starting with special teeth for

cutting and tearing. They also have hunting instincts that make them efficient predators of other animals. They catch fish, eat carrion (usually meat that other predators have killed), and hunt other animals when they are hungry. But most bears are omnivorous – that is, as well as meat, they also eat vegetation. This includes berries, fruits, leaves, shoots, roots and bulbs, even grass. Of all the bears, polar bears are the ones that are mainly hunters and meat-eaters.

Most bears are brown or black, and live in dense forests where dark coats make them almost invisible. Grizzly bears live in more open forests and on the tundra. Polar bears live in the Arctic, on open plains and sea ice.

Of the ten kinds of bears alive today, the biggest measure over 6.5 feet (2 m) from nose to tail and weigh up to 1,500 pounds (680 kg).

The smallest are less than 4 feet (1.2 m) long and weigh up to 200 pounds (90 kg). Even the biggest modern bear is overshadowed in size by the massive "cave bear," one of many species known only as fossils, which lived up to 10,000 years ago.

Getting to know bears

THE BEARS
(see map and outline below)

1 **Eurasian brown bear**
2 **Grizzly bear:** Northern North America
3 **Kodiak bear:** Coastal Alaska
4 **Polar bear:** Arctic and sub-Arctic
5 **Asian black bear:** Kashmir, Nepal, China, Japan
6 **American black bear:** North America
7 **Sloth bear:** Sri Lanka, India
8 **Sun bear:** Burma, Malay Peninsula, Borneo, Sumatra, southern China
9 **Spectacled bear:** Northwestern South America
10 **Giant panda:** China
11 **Cave bear:** Europe and Asia
12 **Siberian brown bear:** North Russia

Bears are curiously appealing to man. We like to think of them as wise, friendly, gentle animals, perhaps like grown-up teddy bears (see p.27). Scientists who have studied them tell another story. Mothers care lovingly for their cubs, which are usually good companions for each other and play together. However, once the cubs reach independence, they quickly grow apart and become strangers to their mother and to each other. Adults are solitary animals that seem to prefer wandering alone. When they meet, they threaten or quarrel with each other, smaller ones always giving way to bigger ones. Even males and females that come together for mating seldom keep company for long.

Giant panda, central China

Cubs reared as pets by man are playful and inquisitive, but soon grow too strong and destructive to live around the house. Caged or tethered, they become bored and aggressive, and have to be released, given to a zoo – or destroyed. In zoos they become lazy, but seldom friendly. Because of their uncertain temper, keepers are always wary of them.

Wild bears can be seen in many parks in the United States. They are seldom aggressive to humans, unless hungry or cross, but visitors are warned very strongly not to feed them or try to reach out to them (p.27). You never know just how hungry or how cross they may be. Even a small bear is very strong for its size, with sharp teeth and claws that can inflict serious damage.

Himalayan brown bear cubs

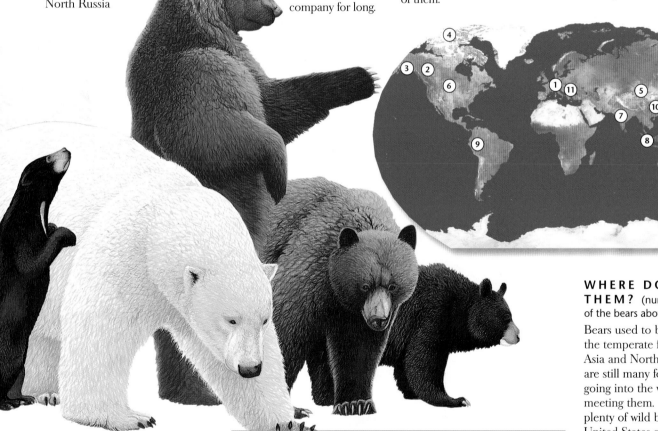

WHERE DO WE SEE THEM? (numbers refer to list of the bears above left)

Bears used to be plentiful in all the temperate forests of Europe, Asia and North America. There are still many folktales about going into the woods and meeting them. Today there are plenty of wild bears in the United States and Canada – they are popular attractions in many forest parks - and in forests of tropical South America and forested areas of Asia. But there are very few left in Europe, where they are found mainly in eastern forests and mountain wildernesses. Polar bears still roam widely in the Arctic.

FOOTPRINTS

If you are in bear country, look out for big, five-toed footprints in snow or mud, and long, deep scratch-marks on the bark of trees. And TAKE CARE. Bears are not fierce hunters, but neither are they friendly to people. If one comes towards you, make the biggest noise you can and back away.

GIANT CAVE BEARS

Ten thousand years ago giant bears, much bigger than any alive today, roamed the forests of Asia and Europe.

FACT FILE

Order:	Carnivora (meat-eaters)
Family:	Ursidae (bears)
Latin name:	*Ursus spelaeus*
Color:	Unknown, probably dark brown
Length:	Up to 10 ft (3 m)
Height:	At shoulder: 4.5 ft (1.4 m)
Weight:	Probably up to 3,300 lb (1,500 kg)
Range:	Southern Europe from southern Britain to Turkey, including northern Spain, Italy and Greece

BEAR TEETH

The earliest bear-like animals were meat-eaters with small pointed (canine) teeth and flesh-cutting (carnassial) teeth in the sides of their jaws, like those of a modern dog. The back teeth (molars) were quite small. Like dogs, they tore and cut up their meaty food and swallowed it in chunks.

As they evolved, cave bears, like modern bears, kept their long, sharp canine teeth (useful in fighting), reduced their cutting carnassials, and developed wide, flat molar teeth (used for grinding vegetable foods).

Bear

Dog

CAVE BEARS

Giant cave bears lived in a wide stretch of forest that covered central and southern Europe, from northern Spain to southern Russia . They died out when brown bears and man arrived to occupy the same area.

THOUGH THE EARLIEST BEARS were as small as the smallest we know today, there soon appeared much bigger forms all over the world. We know a lot about them from their bones and teeth. Bear bones were strong, and made good fossils that have lasted well through the ages.

In Europe especially there arose a very big kind of forest and mountain bear, which first appeared over 200,000 years ago. Thousands of its bones have been found in caves and sheltered corners among rocks all over central Europe. For this reason, we call them 'cave bears'. The scientific name, *Ursus spelaeus*, means much the same.

They probably wintered in caves, as many modern bears do today, and died there during a winter sleep, leaving deep piles of skulls and skeletons for scientists to study. Remains of as many as 30,000 bears have been found in one of the caves, accumulated over tens of thousands of years.

We find bones of cave bears in France, Germany, southern Britain, Spain, Italy and central Europe as far east as Greece. Similar in shape to modern brown bears, cave bears had a larger head with domed forehead. From the length of their bones, we can work out that the biggest stood about 4.8 ft (1.5 m) tall at the shoulder, and over 9.5 ft

How bears began

(3 m) when standing upright – bigger than any other forest mammal alive at that time.

Despite their size, cave bears were not fierce predators. They had grinding rather than flesh-cutting teeth, and seem to have fed mainly on vegetation. They flourished for over 200,000 years, and were still common 30,000 years ago, the time when humans first arrived in Europe. Man hunted them, but that is probably not the main reason why their numbers declined quickly. It was a time when brown bears were spreading, and probably competing with them for food and space. The last cave bears died out about 10,000 years ago.

The earliest-known ancestors of modern bears, now found only as fossil bones, were small, dog-like animals that lived about 20 million years ago. They probably hunted in small family groups on open plains, like the jackals of today. Some took to living in forests, over many thousands of years becoming larger and heavier. Extra size would help them to push their way through thick undergrowth, and protect them from some of the larger predators.

They probably developed denser fur, which allowed them to live in colder climates on mountains and in the northern forests. Their teeth also altered. The cutting teeth on the sides of their jaws became smaller, and the grinding teeth at the back grew larger, suiting them better for a vegetarian diet.

Dozens of different species arose. By 3 million years ago there were some, called *Ursus minimus* ('small bear'), that we would have recognized as true bears. They probably looked something like Malayan sun bears, the smallest of modern bears. From these developed the different kinds of brown and black bears, and the big cave bears shown on these pages.

In the time before man, huge areas that are now grasslands and cities were heavily forested. Animals like bears, adapted to live in forests, could spread almost anywhere in the tropical or temperate world. Among their widely scattered populations arose the many different sizes and color varieties that we see in both brown and black bears. Now man has cleared much of the forest for farming and settlements (p.38), leaving isolated pockets of bears all over the world.

GIANT MAMMALS

Cave bears were just one of many kinds of giant mammals that lived throughout the same period.

■ Giant deer much taller than modern red deer, with antlers 13 ft (4 m) across, were quite common on the plains of Europe.

GIANT DEER

■ Giant rhinoceroses twice as tall as modern ones, with horns 6.5 ft (2 m) long, roamed southern Russia and Europe.

GIANT RHINOCEROS

■ Mammoths, related to modern elephants but some standing almost twice as tall, lived in northern Russia.

MAMMOTH

■ Beavers the size of small cattle lived in rivers of North America.

GIANT BEAVER

■ Giant ground sloths 10 times the weight of modern tree-sloths survived until recent times in Patagonia.

There were small, less spectacular forms as well as big ones – tiny elephants 3 ft (1 m) high and hippos no bigger than large dogs. It was a time of great changes in climate and vegetation. Mammals were adapting by trying out different forms, many of which were just as successful as the ones we know today.

GIANT SLOTH

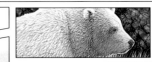

EURASIAN BROWN BEARS

Once they roamed freely across Europe and Asia. Now brown bears survive only in areas that humans cannot use.

FACT FILE

Order:	Carnivora (meat-eaters)
Family:	Ursidae (bears)
Latin name:	*Ursus arctos*
Color:	Varied, pale fawn to dark brown
Length:	Up to 4.6–6 ft. (1.4–1.8 m)
Height:	At shoulder up to 1 m (3.3 ft)
Weight:	Up to 320 kg (700 lb)
Range:	Scandinavia, Russia, central Asia, Syria, Tibet, China, Japan

WHERE DO WE FIND THEM?

Brown bears are still found wherever there is a wide expanse of dense, wilderness forest, and some protection against indiscriminate hunting. In Europe, there are small remnant populations in north-eastern Finland, northern Norway and Sweden, and Estonia, Belarus and western Russia. Further south they live in the Pyrenees, bordering Spain and France, and in the Abruzzi National Park and Trentino Valley of northern Italy. There are larger populations in the mountains of Bosnia-Herzegovina, Yugoslavia, Albania and Macedonia, and a few scattered groups in Hungary, Romania, Slovakia and Poland.

In northern Asia, brown bears are far more plentiful. There are many thousands in the forests of northern Siberia, unknown numbers in northern China and Mongolia, and several thousands in the forests of Hokkaido and other Japanese islands. In southern Asia, they extend, though probably in much smaller numbers, from Syria and Iran through the whole mountainous region to northern India, Pakistan, Afghanistan and Tibet .

IN MEDIEVAL TIMES, when Europe was heavily forested, brown bears and man met frequently on the outskirts of villages and towns. People were usually afraid of them, and made up stories about their strength and fierceness. A bear, it was said, could fell an ox with a single blow, and drag it back to its forest den. Barons and knights used their pictures on shields as symbols of great strength. Bear skins were valued for bedding and wall-hangings. Bear's grease, made from their fat, was a remedy for aches and pains.

The brown bears of Europe and Asia vary greatly in colour, from pale fawn to dark brown. Those of China and Tibet tend to be blue-grey or fawn, while European and Russian bears are more truly brown. But even two cubs from the same litter may be quite different in colour.

Brown bears vary in size, too. Largest are the bears of eastern Siberia (pp.14-15), which are almost the size of Kodiak and large grizzly bears. In comparison, the smallest are much smaller. Brown bears from Syria measure little over 1.5 m (5 ft) and weigh only about 140 kg (300 lb). Because they are small, they are relatively easy to manage, and these are the brown bears that you are most likely to see in European zoos. Russian and American zoos often have the bigger ones, which are more spectacular, but much more costly to keep.

How bears became scarce

BREEDING

Eurasian brown bears mate in May and June. With the first snow in November, the females retire into dens, usually caves or chambers hollowed out in earth banks, and settle to sleep. Two or three cubs are born in January or February, each weighing about 12 oz. (350 g). They feed on milk and they sleep, growing rapidly for eight to ten weeks. In March or April the families emerge, and the young bears forage with their mothers, learning where and how to feed.

Brown bear of the Bavarian forests, Germany

Up to about 10,000 years ago extensive forests covered huge areas of Europe and Asia. In the north were forests of birch, larch, spruce and pine, of the kind we see now in Scandinavia and northern Russia. In the south were forests of oak, ash, beech and other deciduous trees – the kind of forest that still exists patchily all over central and southern Europe.

In all these forests lived brown bears, together with deer, wolves, badgers, beavers and dozens of other kinds of mammals, large and small. The first human populations that spread from Africa into Europe and Asia were hunters, who used the forests without destroying them. They would certainly have hunted bears, which provided warm furs, meat, fat and bones.

When men started to settle and turned to farming, they cut down the trees and cleared the land for crops and grazing.

Brown bears never roam far from the forest

The forests, especially the southern deciduous forests, began to disappear. The animals that lived in them – especially those that killed sheep and cattle – became enemies.

As the human population increased, more and more of the forests were replaced, first by farmlands, then by towns and cities. There was less and less room for bears.

Today most of the southern European forests have gone, and what is left has been subdivided into small areas, many of them too small to support wide-ranging animals. Brown bears, too, have disappeared from most of Europe. Those that remain are subject to government controls. Some stocks are completely protected, others regarded as game animals, of which hunters are permitted to shoot a certain number each year. This is sometimes necessary, to prevent them from becoming a nuisance where forests and farms run close together.

However, huge areas of northern native forests remain in Siberia and other parts of Asia, and brown bears are still plentiful there. In Hokkaido, Japan, large brown bears have for long been a menace to upland farmers, killing dozens of horses and cattle and hundreds of sheep every year.

Eurasian brown bear with three cubs at the entrance to their den

THE LAST BEARS

Brown bears disappeared from Denmark as long as 5,000 years ago. Over the rest of Europe they survived much longer, but died out as forests were replaced by farmland. The last British bears disappeared from southern forests just over 1,000 years ago. The last German bears survived in the forests of Bavaria until 1836. The Swiss killed the last of their bears in about 1904. A few remained in the French Alps until 1937.

Today almost all of the remaining European countries that have forests and mountains keep at least a small remnant population of brown bears. Usually they care for them, and try to protect them from hunters.

SIBERIAN BROWN BEARS

The mountain forests of eastern Siberia are home to the biggest and most prosperous Eurasian bears.

FACT FILE

Order:	Carnivora (meat-eaters)
Family:	Ursidae (bears)
Latin name:	*Ursus arctos*
Color:	Various, yellowish to dark brown
Length:	5.2–6.5 ft. (1.6–2 m)
Height:	At shoulder 3.3 ft. (1 m)
Weight:	Up to 990 lbs. (450 kg)
Range:	Eastern Siberia

BEARS' PARADISE

The cool, damp mountain forests of north-eastern Siberia provide one of the best remaining habitats for Asian brown bears. Human populations are low, and concentrated in the few towns and cities. Except near the settlements, there are not many hunters or foresters, so there is little to disturb the bears in their daily and seasonal living. Here we find some of the largest brown bears – almost as large and heavy as Kodiak bears (pp. 18–19), which live in similar habitats in North America, just across the Pacific Ocean.

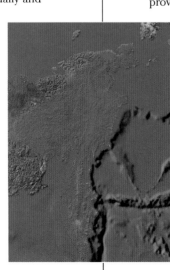

THE KAMCHATKA and Chukotsk peninsulas, in the far eastern corner of Siberia, are mountainous and heavily forested with pine, spruce and birch. Along the coast of the Arctic Ocean the forest thins out, first to taiga (a mixture of open forest, shrubs and grassland) and then to a tundra of low Arctic shrubs. In the forest and taiga, and possibly on the tundra as well, live many thousands of Siberian brown bears, including some of the largest in all Asia.

These are not a separate species. They are just bears that seem fortunate enough to be living in almost ideal conditions for brown bears – conditions that allow them to grow to full size, and to build up to high densities of population. This is the home, too, of many other forest animals, including several species of deer, and the rivers run rich with salmon during the autumn spawning.

We cannot be sure why this habitat is so ideal for brown bears. But it seems to provide plenty of food throughout spring, summer and autumn, and plenty of warm, comfortable places for their winter sleep. Their most critical time of year is autumn, when they need to fatten in preparation for wintering. The abundance of fish and berries in July and August, sometimes as late as September, must be very important to them, ensuring a sound, winter-long sleep and safe awakening in spring.

Siberian calendar

HOW MANY BEARS PER SQUARE MILE?

Brown bears need a huge area for hunting. In many forests of the world each bear needs at least 10−20 sq. mi. (25−50 km²), which it patrols constantly to find enough food for itself. So, in an area of 200 sq. mi. (500 km²), you might expect to find between 10 and 20 bears − more or less, depending on the amount of food available for them.

In the forests of Kamchatka, Russian scientists have recorded five times as many bears in areas of this size, and in some places up to twenty times as many, all large, fat and healthy. The most favored areas are river valleys where the fishing is particularly good. This suggests that salmon are a very important part of the bears' diet, if only for a few weeks each year. They certainly help to build up the stores of fat that the bears need to see them through their long winter sleep.

◄ WINTER

Winters are long in this part of the world. Snow covers the ground for four or five months, and food is scarce. In late October and November the bears find dens or sheltered places − in caves, hollows between rocks, under boulders or fallen trees, in caverns scratched out in riverbanks. Each bear finds a place of its own, possibly one where it has wintered before. It brings in a thick carpet of dried ferns, branches, leaves and grasses, then settles in to sleep. Whatever the weather outside, however cold or rainy, however strong the winds or heavy the snow, with luck the sleeping bear remains undisturbed until March.

SPRING

Male bears are the first to leave their dens in April, followed a few days later by the females with their cubs. It is still cold, and there is little food about. But they scrape through the last of the snow to find berries, rose hips, pine cones and dried grass. There may also be dead salmon, or the carcasses of reindeer, elk or other animals that died during the winter. After a week or two come the first spring shoots of herbs and grasses, and opening buds of trees and shrubs − all good fodder for hungry bears. Some that live near the coast may forage on the beaches for washed-up fish, seals or even whales.

◄ SUMMER

From June the grasses and herbs grow quickly, putting out shoots that are rich in sugars and proteins. Shrubs and trees develop new growth, which the bears munch happily, grinding the soft stems with their broad molar teeth. Young trees provide nourishing bark, which they tear off in strips with their sharp claws. Now the ground is soft enough to dig for roots, ants' nests and the burrows and dens of mice, lemmings, ground squirrels and other small rodents. Ground-nesting ducks and geese provide tasty, nutritious eggs, and young deer become plentiful.

DO BEARS HIBERNATE?

Several kinds of animals sleep during the winter, but there are differences in the way they sleep. Dormice and other small mammals go into a deep sleep, in which they allow their body temperature to fall almost to that of their surroundings. It takes several hours for them to warm up and awaken. This is called "hibernation." Bears go into a much lighter sleep, in which the body temperature falls only very slightly, if at all. If disturbed, they can wake up and become active within minutes. This is called "dormancy," not hibernation. If a bear could hibernate, letting its body temperature fall, it would lose less heat and save energy over the winter months. But it would need several days to warm up and become efficient, and be very much at risk from predators while doing so.

Siberian brown bear with her cub

AUTUMN

Summers are short. By July much of the growth is over, and seeds, berries and other fruit are forming. These, too, are good food for bears. But bears that live close to rivers and streams spend their waking hours fishing, for this is the time when salmon and char come up the rivers to spawn. Bears forget their quarrels and rivalries and line up along the banks, grabbing salmon with their teeth, and scooping them from the water with their paws. This lasts for five to six weeks. When the salmon run is over, there is still time to feed on berries and fruit before winter sets in.

GRIZZLY BEARS

The great gray-brown bears of America's northwest forest and tundra. Even the young ones have gray-tipped fur.

FACT FILE

Order:	Carnivora (meat-eaters)
Family:	Ursidae (bears)
Latin name:	*Ursus horribilis*
Color:	Various, yellowish to gray-brown
Length:	5.2–6.5 ft. (1.6–2 m)
Height:	At shoulder 3.3 ft. (1 m)
Weight:	Up to 880 lbs. (400 kg)
Range:	Alaska, northwestern Canada, Rocky Mountains of United States

WHAT IS A GRIZZLY BEAR?

Grizzly bears are the brown bears of North America. Some scientists think that they are no different from brown bears of Asia and Europe, and should have the same name, *Ursus arctos*. Others think that, not only do they differ from brown bears elsewhere, but there are as many as 80 different kinds of grizzly bears in different parts of North America, each a species or subspecies in its own right.

They may be any color from pale fawn to near-black. Generally they are larger and shaggier than black bears. In profile their face is concave (like a dish), giving them a high forehead and slightly turned-up nose, and their shoulders have a distinctive hump.

WHERE DO THEY LIVE?

Look out for grizzly bears in Alaska, the Yukon and Northwest Territories, on Banks Island in the Canadian Arctic, in British Columbia, western Alberta, and the Rocky Mountain states of the United States south to New Mexico. In the south they live mainly in dense mountain forest, emerging onto grasslands and river floodplains. In the treeless north they are found on tundra, often living close to rivers that provide good fishing in spring and summer.

EARLY AMERICAN SETTLERS from Europe, trekking westwards through the forests of the Rocky Mountain foothills, began to meet large brown bears. They were bigger and more woolly than the American black bears (pp. 26–27) that were already familiar to them, and similar to the brown bears they had left behind in the forests of Europe.

Although they ranged in color from pale tan to dark brown or near-black, they often had long, gray-tipped hairs called "guard hairs" in their coat that gave them an all-over grayish or "grizzled" appearance. Their size and grayish fur at first suggested that they might just be old bears, but that soon proved wrong. Even the young, half-grown animals showed the characteristic gray tips. So the settlers called them grizzly bears (grizzly means gray-haired). Later, explorers and gold-mining prospectors who traveled north beyond the forest were surprised to find these same large, gray-brown bears wandering over the tundra.

Grizzlies are big, heavy, lumbering bears that usually sleep during the day and come out to forage at night. Adults are mostly solitary. Several may gather together round a source of food – perhaps a stretch of river where the salmon or char are jumping – but otherwise they tend to keep out of each other's way. Occasionally pairs are seen together at mating time, in June or July. Often a single female attracts two or three males, who follow her at a distance, quarreling and fighting among themselves. This is when you are most likely to hear them roaring and growling.

Both males and females fatten during summer and autumn, laying down stores of fat under their skin and inside their abdomen. As the weather turns colder, they find caves or dig dens for themselves in a hillside, where they can settle to sleep. Both sexes sleep for three or four months each winter, sometimes more, living on their stored fat.

FEEDING

In spring, when grizzly bears emerge from sleep, they patrol an area of several square miles, finding where the food is good and returning on a circuit every few days. They eat shoots and leaves, and tear trees apart to munch the soft, sweet, mineral-rich layers under the bark.

Young grizzlies cooling off in a river

Other sources of food include insects, lizards, birds and their eggs, small mammals and dead animals. They listen for wild bees, and climb or push over trees to reach their nests, feasting on larvae, beeswax and honey.

In rivers they forage under stones for shellfish, and catch salmon as they move upriver to breed. Young bears may move fast enough to catch young deer, but older ones are usually too clumsy. If their feeding area includes a farm, grizzly bears occasionally take cattle or sheep. The early settlers killed many grizzlies to protect their stocks of farm animals.

In autumn or fall they scavenge around bird colonies, seeking fat nestlings that cannot yet fly, and search the forests and tundra for berries and fruits, which they munch continuously. This is a critical time for grizzlies. If they cannot find enough food, they may awake from winter sleep to find themselves starving.

Grizzly bear standing up to see more clearly

Where can we see grizzly bears?

Though grizzly bears were once plentiful all over western North America, hunting and forest clearance have reduced their range. Today park rangers and hunters know most about them.

Photographers lining up their cameras on grizzly bears, Alaska

Grizzlies are regular visitors to some of the national parks, and each year a few are killed under licence by hunters, for sport or to protect cattle and sheep. Yellowstone National Park, in Wyoming, Montana and Idaho, has a flourishing population of grizzly bears. Park authorities try to keep in touch with them, mainly to ensure that visitors can travel and camp safely in the park. The bears are active from late spring to late autumn, and generally more likely to wander at night than during the day. Campers are warned not to leave food or rubbish exposed where bears will find it.

For a time the rubbish dump just outside the town of West Yellowstone, in Montana, was a good place to see grizzlies. When food became scarce in late summer and fall, as many as 20 at a time would visit, rummaging for scraps among the rubbish. This became dangerous when the bears started wandering into the town. The problem was solved by creating a new dump some distance away, and surrounding it with a bear-proof fence.

Grizzlies are plentiful too in Glacier National Park, British Columbia, and in many other parks and reserves among the western mountains, in Alaska, and on the barren grounds of northern Canada.

GRIZZLY BEARS' PICNIC

If you go looking for grizzly bears, take great care. However gentle or friendly they appear, they are usually hungry and looking for food. You could become their next meal. Follow the advice of the park authorities. Do not feed them; do not leave food for them; above all, do not take risks with them.

KODIAK BEARS

Largest of all the bears, they live in cool, damp forests of the Alaskan coast, where they feed well on the summer salmon.

FACT FILE

Order:	Carnivora (meat-eaters)
Family:	Ursidae (bears)
Latin name:	*Ursus middendorffi*
Color:	Varied, typically brown
Length:	8.5–10 ft. (2.6–3 m)
Height:	At shoulder up to 4.5 ft. (1.4 m)
Weight:	Up to 1,720 lbs. (780 kg)
Range:	Kodiak Island and neighboring coastal regions of Alaska

WHAT ARE KODIAK BEARS?

They are a kind of brown bear that lives along the southern coast of Alaska and on Kodiak Island and smaller neighboring islands. Though very similar to grizzly bears, they tend to be larger. Males are usually bigger than females, though some mature females can be very big too – just like people.

WHERE CAN WE SEE THEM?

Kodiak Island and the southern coast of Alaska are heavily forested, but there are small coastal towns and fishing settlements where visitors can stay, and wildlife reserves and refuges where they can see bears, especially during the salmon run in July and August.

L IKE THE BROWN BEARS of Europe and Asia, Kodiak bears are animals that live quiet, lonely lives in dense forest and heathland. Close kin to grizzly bears (and said by some scientists to be just another kind of brown bear), they inhabit a coastal strip of Alaska and a nearby group of islands – Kodiak Island and its neighbors. There is little remarkable about them except their size. Big Kodiak bears are the biggest of all bears alive today.

They have also been well studied by scientists, who have watched them, studied their social behavior and tagged them with numbered labels to identify them as individuals. They were some of the first bears to be fitted with radio-transmitting collars, and to have their movements tracked across the very difficult, mountainous country that is their home.

Like all other brown bears, Kodiak bears spend three to four months of every winter, from November to March, asleep in their dens. Mothers produce their two or three cubs in January, emerging with them as the earth begins to warm, and wandering in their company for one or two years. So the cubs learn what they need to know – what foods are good, what skills are required, where danger lies.

Males live alone, playing no part in family life. Like the females, they patrol huge feeding areas, on average 5 sq. mi. (13 km²) in extent, keeping apart for much of the year. Only in July and August, when the salmon come up the rivers to spawn, do Kodiak bears – males and females, cubs and immature animals – meet at the good fishing places to feast and fatten.

Kodiak bears live in a habitat similar to that of Siberian brown bears, and follow a similar calendar (see p.15).

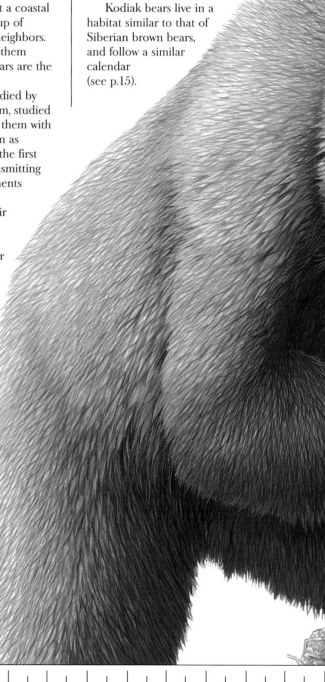

Behavior: how bears live together

Kodiak bear roaring to keep other bears away from his feeding ground

KEEPING APART

Unlike wolves and other hunting carnivores, bears tend to live alone. Exceptions are mothers with cubs, who travel with their families for a year or more, and females ready for mating, whose scent attracts males to them – though only for a few days.

One reason for their solitary behavior is that, for parts of every year, food is scarce. In several square miles of forest there are roots and berries enough for only one bear at a time. So they keep out of each other's way. Like dogs, they use urine to mark out their territories, and probably also use scent glands in their paws and skin. Bears have a sharp sense of smell, and always know where other bears have been. Even humans, walking through the forest, can smell where a bear has scratched or rubbed repeatedly.

When food becomes abundant, as during a salmon run, a dozen or more Kodiak bears often gather at the same place – possibly a shallow patch of river or waterfall where fishing is easy. How do they share this source of food without quarreling? Constant fighting would waste time and energy and cause serious injuries. Instead they use a code of behavior that avoids quarrels and that all seem to understand.

Their code is based on size, sex and age. Large mature males are dominant. This means that

Keeping apart: brown bears fishing for salmon

others give way to them almost without question. Large mature females are next in importance, followed by young males and young females. They decide which is dominant by signals. If two large males meet at a good fishing point that both want to use, they open their jaws, curl back their lips and snarl. After a few moments, one usually drops its head or turns away, and slowly backs off. The contest is over. If not, they fight briefly with teeth, claws and angry growls, until one or other moves away.

The importance of size as the sign of dominance may help to explain why Kodiak bears are big. If big animals get the best fishing places, and the best chances of fattening for the winter, then it pays to be big. Large bears will have better chances of survival, produce more offspring, and ensure that, at least in that area, there will be more large bears than small in future generations.

Bears cannot talk. But scientists who study their

behavior have found a wide range of signals – ears forward or back, body sideways or head on, head up, down or sideways, mouth open or closed, neck stretched or shortened – that other bears interpret just as though they were spoken messages. If you are watching bears with this in mind, after a time you too will be able to understand the messages that they pass to each other without words.

Young brown bears play-fighting

CALENDAR

Early spring is the thin time of year. Kodiak bears emerge from their dens, hungry after months of fasting, to a world of uncertain weather and little to eat. Late spring, summer and autumn bring months of plenty – a succession of foods, from fresh new shoots to green leaves, from fat salmon to nourishing berries and seeds.

Autumn is the time when every bear, big or small, must fatten up for the long winter ahead. Those that fail to fatten are unlikely to survive. But there are many thousands of Kodiak bears. Their size and numbers show that this corner of the world is kind to them.

POLAR BEARS

Second-biggest of all the bears, yellowish-white with black eyes and noses, polar bears live in the far north, along the shores of the Arctic Ocean and neighboring cold seas.

FACT FILE

Order:	Carnivora (meat-eaters)
Family:	Ursidae (bears)
Latin name:	*Thalarctos maritimus*
Color:	White to pale yellow
Length:	Males 7–8 ft. (2–2.5 m)
Height:	At shoulder 5 ft. (1.6 m)
Weight:	Males 770–1,500 lbs. (350–650 kg) or more, females 330–530 lbs. (150–250 kg), occasionally as much as 1,100 lbs. (500 kg)
Range:	Shores and sea ice of the Arctic Ocean and neighboring seas

WHERE DO THEY LIVE?

Polar bears live mainly along the shores of the Arctic Ocean and neighboring seas, especially where the ice breaks and the sea is open in winter (see map). In summer they wander on land, though never far from the sea. In early winter, when the sea ice forms again, they travel over it, often leaving the land far behind. Polar bears have been seen within a few miles of the North Pole.

WHERE DO THEY FEED?

Polar bears feed mostly at sea. They can walk and run over the ice, but they are also strong swimmers. On the ice they catch young seals, including walruses, and they dive from the ice edge to catch small whales in the water. In summer they come ashore to feed on grass, mosses and berries. They catch birds on their nests, take eggs, scoop salmon, char and other fish from the streams, and hunt for dead animals. A dead whale or seal washed up on shore provides a feast for hungry bears.

THOUGH CLOSELY RELATED to grizzlies, polar bears could never be mistaken for any other kind of bear. Except for their noses, eyes and claws, they are white (sometimes very pale golden yellow) all over. Living only in the Arctic, they spend much of their time on the sea ice or along the shore. In summer, when the inshore sea ice has melted, they wander inland to hunt and scavenge for food.

Fully grown males are almost as large as Kodiak bears. Standing on four legs they are almost chest-high to a tall man. Rearing up on their hind legs, they can reach up to 13 feet (4 m). Females are smaller, but still larger than the largest lions or tigers. Half-grown cubs stand as tall as a man. Often, like the two in the picture, they rear up to wrestle, hug and bite each other in friendly play.

Polar bears are solitary animals. If you see two or three together, it is usually a mother with her half-grown cubs. Adults very seldom gather, except at a carcass − a dead animal on which they are feeding. When two or three come together, they usually quarrel, and the strongest drives the others away.

People who live where there are polar bears try to keep out of their way. They are very big, very strong, and always hungry. They are not friendly to humans, and can be **very dangerous.**

Polar bear mother with two young cubs

Living in the Arctic

Polar bears live in a thick furry blanket

DENSE FUR

The dense white fur, up to 1 ft. (30 cm) thick, acts as an insulating blanket, keeping the wind out and the bear's own body heat in. In summer it acts also as a greenhouse. Sunlight shines through the upper layers and warms the lower layers close to the skin, helping the bear to keep warm. In warm summer weather, polar bears easily become overheated, especially if they are active. After running even a short distance they have to stop, pant and lie down to cool off.

The fur is dense and oily enough to keep water from the skin. When a polar bear emerges from the sea, only the long outer fur is wet. The water freezes - and the bear shakes it off in a shower of ice crystals.

M any brown and grizzly bears live in extreme cold in winter. Polar bears live year-round in the Arctic. How do they survive when it is cold all the time?

They have several ways of dealing with cold. Though the Arctic can be very cold in winter, with air temperatures down to -22°F (-30°C), no sunshine, and strong winds that make the air feel colder, in summer it can be quite mild. Even with air temperatures close to freezing point, dry soils, rocks, plants and animals heat up in the sun. There are still strong winds, which whisk up the snow and whirl it around, but it is usually possible to find sheltered corners where everything feels warm.

Polar bears are very well insulated against cold. Under their thick fur and hide is a layer of fat, which helps to keep them warm and acts as a food store too. Pregnant females spend their winters sleeping in dens, well away from the weather. Other bears winter on the sea ice, which is cold, but warmer than the land. So long as they keep moving and feed occasionally, they are able to keep warm.

In summer, keeping warm is seldom a problem for polar bears. Often they become too hot in the sun, and have to cool off by sprawling in the snow or taking a swim.

To keep them from slipping when walking on ice and snow, polar bears have huge feet with horny pads and sharp nails. These grip the ice and spread their weight over it. Fresh footprints in the snow are more than 1 foot (30 cm) across.

SWIMMING

All bears can swim, but polar bears are especially good swimmers. Their dense, double-layered fur coat is almost waterproof, keeping the cold seawater off their skin. The huge feet act as paddles, pushing them steadily through the water.

In a dive, polar bears can hold their breath for more than a minute. Though they cannot swim fast enough to catch seals in the water, often they swim between ice floes, looking out for seals asleep on the ice. They approach quietly, then leap out in a flurry to catch them.

HIDING

S eals lying on the ice keep an eye open for prowling bears. With their all-white fur, polar bears are well camouflaged, except for their black eyes and noses. Early travelers reported that, when hunting seals, a bear would carry a piece of ice to hide its black nose, so the seals would not see it.

WANDERERS OF THE NORTH

Polar bears are not easy to study, but a big international research project has told us a lot about where and how they live.

HOW MANY POLAR BEARS?

Wandering widely across the Arctic, with seldom more than two or three together, and well camouflaged against their background of ice and snow, polar bears are very hard to count. Biologists who study them estimate about

■ 5,000 in the Barents Sea, Greenland Sea and Svalbard area
■ 5,000 along the Siberian coast
■ up to 7,000 north of Bering Strait
■ 8,000 in the Canadian Arctic
■ 2,000 off northern Alaska
■ and possibly 1,000 around the Greenland coasts

These are all low estimates. A likely total is 30,000−40,000.

Polar bear enjoying a swim

HOW LONG DO THEY LIVE?

It is hard, too, to tell the age of a polar bear, once it has reached full size. One way is to count rings of growth in their big canine teeth, which continue to grow throughout life − rather like rings in a tree trunk. Another is to tag animals when they are cubs, and keep records throughout their lives.

One in every four or five cubs dies during its first summer. Some are killed and eaten by male bears. This is why mothers usually keep away from where the males are hunting. Many young adults are slow to learn the skills that a polar bear needs to live in the Arctic. They die, usually of starvation, before they are five or six. Bears that reach ages of 10 or more have learned how to survive, and often live to their late 20s. Some of the oldest polar bears known have been more than 30 years old.

THOUGH THEY ARE FOUND all over the Arctic, polar bears live mostly on sea ice, especially along the coasts where new ice forms each year. They particularly like groups of islands, with channels where the currents are strong and the waters rich in plankton and fish, and "polynyas" − areas where the ice is moving and likely to have cracks even in winter. Here they find the young seals that are their favourite food.

Because polar bears look very much alike wherever we find them, we used to think that they all roamed widely all over the Arctic. But research has shown otherwise. Biologists have been catching and marking individual bears, and fitting some with collars that transmit radio signals so their movements can be tracked by satellites. Now we know that, though polar bears may wander several hundred miles in the course of a year, they tend to stay in, or return to, the area where they were born.

If they drift southwards with sea ice, they walk back to where they started. If they roam widely in search of food, they are most likely to follow a circular track that, after weeks or months, brings them back to a home area. This is more efficient than just wandering anywhere. It gives them a chance to learn where to find food at different times of the year, and which areas to avoid.

Polar bears and man

Mothers with cubs may walk long distances in search of food

NAVIGATION

Radio-tracking has shown that some individuals wander much more widely than others. Some have traveled between Svalbard and Greenland, others from Svalbard to the Russian coast. A mother with two cubs walked from eastern Greenland to Franz Josef Land, almost 600 miles (1,000 km) in less than a month. Others have traveled on the pack ice from Wrangel Island, off the northeastern Siberian coast, to Alaska, covering 25–50 miles (40–80 km) per day. How do they navigate over such long distances and find their way home? We do not know.

Towns and smaller settlements in the Arctic are often visited by polar bears, especially in summer when natural foods are scarce. Bears learn quickly, and many have learned that town trash cans and garbage dumps often contain food. So they come in to scavenge.

People in the town get nervous about them, and call in the police. A few years ago scavenging bears were shot. Today they are more likely to be drugged and carried to the local bear jail. Then they are transported out of town by truck or helicopter.

Scavenging bears are usually young ones that are hungry and not good at hunting elsewhere. Some

Mother and half-grown cub investigating a truck

come back time after time for a good meal at the dump. A few settlements make their scavenging bears a tourist attraction. Visitors can see them in jail, or wandering at night in the glow of truck headlights.

They often visit isolated shacks and trappers' huts, again in search of food. Once polar bears get the idea that there is food inside a hut, very little can be done to keep them out. With claws and teeth they break down doors, pull apart walls and rip open boxes and cans.

INTERNATIONAL PROTECTION

Polar bears have always been hunted, usually in small numbers, by native peoples of the Arctic, for their furs and meat. In the last 200 years, far more have been trapped and shot so their furs could be sold. More recently they have been hunted by sportsmen looking for trophy skins to hang on their wall or make into mats.

Though nobody knew how many bears there were, so many were taken that their numbers were almost certainly decreasing. In 1965, scientists of the five nations that were mainly responsible for the Arctic – Canada, Denmark (for Greenland), Norway, the United States and the USSR – met to find out what research was being done on polar bears.

In 1973, after a lot of discussion, the five nations signed a joint agreement, the International Agreement on the Conservation of Polar Bears and their Habitat, to protect the bears and the places where they live. All the nations agreed to set up research projects to find out how many bears there were, how many were being hunted and how they could best be managed.

This agreement is still operating. Though some bears are still hunted each year, mostly by native peoples for their own use, the stocks

as a whole are much better protected than they ever were before. Many of the places where they live are now protected, too, so the bears are left in peace.

CATCHING A POLAR BEAR

Scientists catch their bears by shooting them with a drug-filled syringe, fired from a shotgun. This is often done from a helicopter. The needle has to be long enough to penetrate the fur, the tough skin and the layer of blubber (fat) beneath, so that the drug is injected into the rump or shoulder muscles. After five to ten minutes the bear staggers and falls down, then goes into a deep sleep for about an hour.

That gives the scientists a chance to weigh it, measure it, examine it for scars and injuries, fit it with a numbered ear-tag, tattoo the same number inside its mouth (in case the tag is lost), and perhaps fit it with a radio-collar. Then they inject it with an antidote to the drug – and get back into the helicopter before the bear wakes up.

Scientists examining a drugged polar bear

FAMILY LIFE

No bigger than small rabbits at birth, polar bear cubs are born in mid-winter. Helpless and without fur, they live in a dark den, burrowed in a snowbank.

COURTSHIP AND MATING

A female polar bear whose cubs have grown up and left is usually ready to mate again in spring, about late April or May. She produces a particular scent attractive to males, which carries for long distances on the wind. Several males may be attracted. When they find her, they travel with her for a few days, fighting each other off and mating with her. Then her scent disappears, and they all go their own separate ways. So polar bear fathers never meet their cubs, or play any part in bringing them up.

Male bears sniff the air to catch the scent of females that are ready to mate

I N OCTOBER, EACH PREGNANT female polar bear seeks a den, usually ashore but sometimes on the sea ice, where she can hide away undisturbed for the winter. On land she looks for snowdrifts or banks of soft earth on the sides of hills, usually within a few miles of the sea. On sea ice she may find a natural cave, formed from sheets of ice lifted sideways by pressure and covered with snow. Each female digs into the snow, making a snug shelter about 6.5 feet (2 m) long and 3.3 feet (1 m) wide and high. She may try several before finally settling. Then she curls up and goes to sleep.

Enough air filters through the snow for her to breathe without difficulty. Whatever the weather outside, the den stays comfortable, warmed slightly by the sleeping bear. Her body temperature falls slightly, usually not more than about 9°F (5°C). She has no need for food. She lives on the store of body fat that she built up during summer and autumn.

In December, she gives birth to her cubs, usually two. Covered with fine hair and tiny, they are about 1 foot (30 cm) long, and weigh no more than 21–28 ounces (600–800 g). She wakes up long enough to lick them clean and make sure that they find her teats. Then she goes back to sleep. The cubs too spend much of their time sleeping, waking from time to time to feed on warm, creamy milk.

Females start to breed when they are 4–5 years old and continue until they are 20 or more. Females fight less than males, and so tend to live longer.

The polar bear's calendar

GROWING CUBS

Mothers open the dens in March or April and emerge with their cubs. By this time the cubs, three to four months old, weigh 22–33 lbs. (10–15 kg), and are strong enough to roll, play and slide in the snow. After a few days the families are ready to move away, usually onto the sea ice. The cubs continue to feed from their mothers, but gradually learn how to hunt and scavenge for themselves. The families stay together for 18 months to two years or longer. After that the cubs move away to live independently, and the mothers seek another mating.

Mothers and cubs stay together for up to two years, sometimes longer

DELAYED DEVELOPMENT

When a polar bear has mated, the fertilized eggs do not start to develop immediately. If they did, the cubs would be born in early winter – quite the wrong time of year. The eggs settle in the wall of the mother's uterus in about August, then start to grow and develop. Meanwhile the mothers-to-be have to hunt constantly, eating and growing fat. Each has to put on about 440 lbs. (200 kg) of fat to be sure of being able to last and to feed the cubs through the winter. They do this mainly by feeding on young, fat seals, which they catch on the pack ice.

Winters in the Arctic are long and cold. For six to nine or more months each year the sea is frozen over, the land covered with snow. Food is difficult to find. Polar bears cannot get together or stay in the same place for long. They would quickly run out of things to eat. Instead they live solitary lives, moving continuously in a constant search for food.

Cubs stay with their mothers at least a year and a half, usually more, before they have learnt enough to be able to hunt for themselves. Females cannot breed every year, only every second or third year. In late autumn or winter, when food is very scarce, females sleep for weeks on end to save energy.

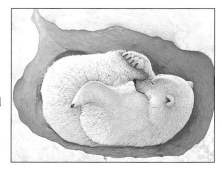

AUTUMN

In October, female polar bears that are pregnant move ashore, where they dig lairs or "dens" for themselves in the snowbanks. Sheltered from cold winds, they sleep continuously, awaiting the arrival of their pups.

Males and nonpregnant females remain active, move out onto the sea ice and hunt where they can. The sea is usually warmer than the land, and provides better chances of finding food.

EQUIPPED FOR THE COLD WINDS

The white fur has a thick underpelt of short hairs, and much longer "guard hairs." In the sun this double layer acts as a greenhouse, keeping the wind out and trapping the sun's heat close to the skin. In winter, the bears have a layer of blubber under the skin that provides a food store and helps to keep them warm.

WINTER

Pregnant females ashore in their dens produce one, two or three pups (usually two) between November and early January, feeding them on rich milk.

Males and nonpregnant females winter on the sea ice, seeking breathing holes and "leads" (cracks in the ice) where seals come up to breathe. When a seal puts its nose through the ice, the bear crashes down to grab it before it can escape.

SPRING

Mothers emerge from their dens with their pups, which are now big enough to walk and run. The mothers hunt for food, and the pups learn by example what is good to eat. Females with pups tend to stay on land, out of the way of males. Those without pups move out onto sea ice to seek a mate. Mating pairs stay together for a week or more, then separate. Males wander over the sea ice until it becomes too soft to hold them, then move in towards land.

SUMMER

Food for polar bears, never plentiful on land, is often particularly scarce in summer. Males and females that are ashore spend a lot of time resting in temporary dens, keeping cool and saving energy. Those that are out on the pack ice have better chances of feeding, and spend their summers fattening up.

FACT FILE

Order:	Carnivora (meat-eaters)
Family:	Ursidae (bears)
Latin name:	*Euarctos americanus*
Color:	Variable, pale silver-gray to black
Length:	4.6–6 ft. (1.4–1.8 m)
Height:	At shoulder 2.5 ft. (75 cm)
Weight:	Up to 485 lbs. (220 kg)
Range:	Alaska, Canada, western and central United States, New England, Florida, northern Mexico

SOLITARY BEARS

Black bears, like most other bears, live most of their lives alone. Males and females come together only briefly to mate, then wander off alone. They go to ground in winter, sleeping in dens during the hardest months when food is scarce. Mothers give birth to two or three cubs, each weighing about 1 lb. (500 g). The cubs stay with their mothers for about 18 months, then go their separate ways.

WHERE DO WE FIND THEM?

The early settlers used to find black bears in all the forested areas of North America. Now much of the forest has been cut down, but where it survives there are still plenty of black bears. Hunting has made them timid, and they live mainly well away from towns and people. The best places to see them are forests of the national and state parks and reserves.

AMERICAN BLACK BEARS

Lords of the forests, they are still plentiful in well-timbered areas of the United States and Canada.

THE FORESTS THAT FORMERLY covered so much of North America were home to both brown and black bears. Both penetrated deep among the trees and thickets, but brown bears also used the open spaces along the riverbanks and the grasslands around the forest margins. When people began to enter the forests and clear them for farmland, they started by clearing the open ground – the river plains and forest edges, where brown bears hunted and played. When they needed more land, they burned and cut the denser forest too. That is when black bears began to lose their homes.

Though neither species is as plentiful as in earlier times, black bears remain more widespread than brown. They can be seen in well over half the states of the United States, and many of the heavily forested states have enough of them to allow licensed hunting with dogs and guns. They are plentiful, too, in Canada's extensive forests.

Black bears feel safest with trees around them. When danger threatens, small cubs run to hide in the darkest corner they can find, usually under a fallen trunk or among the roots. Larger cubs that are too big to hide, and young bears, scramble up the nearest tree and "freeze" among the branches. Young bears climb just for fun, too, using the limbs and branches as trapezes, sometimes feeding on leaves and shoots, often just watching the world from a place of safety. Older bears grow too fat and heavy to climb, but by then they are big enough to face most dangers on the ground.

They feed on roots, leaves, shoots, young growing plants, berries, birds' eggs and, occasionally, carrion (dead animals). They love honey and fruit. Mothers rearing young cubs introduce them to different kinds of food in turn. That is how the cubs learn what is good to eat and what to avoid.

BRINGING UP BEAR CUBS

Biologists who found two orphaned eight-week-old black bear cubs took them home and fed them first on cows' milk sweetened with honey. After two or three weeks the cubs accepted chopped canned peaches and baby-foods, then more solid apples and leaves. At six weeks they enjoyed oatmeal sweetened with honey and fruit syrup. Though not at first interested in raw meat, they liked to chew frankfurter sausages and bones, and later took to minced beef and fish. In three months their weight rose from 2.2 lbs. (1 kg) to about 30 lbs. (13–14 kg).

They enjoyed taking showers and playing in the bath, and got into mischief, hiding in dark cupboards and laundry hampers, toppling chairs and play-fighting all over the house. They were friendly to their foster-parents, but wary of strangers.

Teddy bears take their name from Theodore Roosevelt, who was President of the United States (1901–09). He was a popular president, whom everyone called "Teddy." He loved outdoor life and was a keen naturalist and hunter. In 1902, while hunting in the

woods, he found a small black bear cub and took it home with him as a pet. A New York toy-maker who heard about "Teddy" Roosevelt's pet bear cub started making and selling stuffed toy bears, which he called "teddy bears" after the president. They became very popular, first in America, then all over the world. Thousands are still made every year, and teddy bears are still among the most loved of all children's toys.

Young black bears play-fighting

Visiting black bears

Though black bears normally avoid places where there are people, in almost every national park and reserve a few of them learn that people bring food. They rummage through rubbish bins, eating the hamburgers,

Black bear with a salmon

sandwiches and buns that visitors throw away. Often they damage the bins. Occasionally they choke to death on cans and plastic bags.

They gather, too, in parking lots, where visitors like to feed them. This is usually forbidden, because it is DANGEROUS. Though black bears are not normally aggressive towards people, their "table manners" can be rough. They may grab food with teeth or claws, or knock over someone they think has food in a pocket or knapsack.

Don't expect to teach good manners to hungry bears. If you feed them in a place like this, you are training them to expect food, and they develop bad habits. They may hurt you, or be rough with someone who comes along later. Then they may have to be shot because they have become dangerous. This is why you are asked not to feed them at all.

Cubs learn woodcraft during their first months of life

WHAT IS A BLACK BEAR?

Smaller and lighter in weight than brown bears, black bears are still large, chunky animals, with solid builds and strong muscles. Their coats are smooth, and vary in color from almost black to almost white. Generally, those of the eastern United States are darker than those of the West, with the palest of all in western Canada. Some "black" bears in Alaska are silvery gray.

One population living near Yakutat Bay is called the "blue" or "glacier" bear, and some biologists consider it a separate subspecies. Whatever the coat color, the muzzle (nose) is usually tan, and there is often a white patch on the chest. Seen sideways, black bears have a convex profile quite different from the concave profile of brown bears.

ASIAN BLACK BEARS

More people, more farms and cities, and less forest leaves these bears with fewer places to hide from humans.

FACT FILE

Order:	Carnivora (meat-eaters)
Family:	Ursidae (bears)
Latin name:	Selenarctos thibetanus
Color:	Various, black, brown and gray
Length:	4.6–5.6 ft. (1.4–1.7 m)
Height:	At shoulder 2.3 ft. (70 cm)
Weight:	Up to 280 lbs. (130 kg)
Range:	Southern and eastern Asia, from northern Iran to Japan

WHAT DO THEY LOOK LIKE?

They are black, brown, reddish brown or dark gray, usually with a brown muzzle – in fact, very much like American black bears, though slightly smaller. They have bigger ears than most other bears, and a long, shaggy coat, often thickest around the shoulders. Nearly all have a white chin, and a white chevron (V-shape) across their chest, like a new moon – hence their alternative name, "moon-bear."

WHERE DO WE FIND THEM?

These are bears of mountain forests. They live in some of the wildest and most remote regions of central and eastern Asia. You might meet them in the wild if you visit the mountains of northern Iran or Afghanistan, the Himalayas of northern Pakistan, India, Nepal and Bhutan, or distant corners of Burma, China, Korea, Laos and Japan.
But you will need to travel with guides who know where to find them. Sadly, in some of these countries you are more likely to see them in captivity, caged or being led through the towns and villages as performing bears.

THE BLACK BEARS OF ASIA are closely related to those of North America, and many biologists group them under the same species name. But they are more uniform in color, and often smaller and lighter in weight.

Their smaller size may be because fewer Asian bears live in rich lowland forests. Formerly their forests were far more extensive, covering huge areas of lowland plains as well as mountains and uplands. Today most of the lowland forest and richer upland forest has been cut down, to be replaced by fields and human settlements. All that is left are the mountain forests, where living conditions are harsher, and smaller bears fare better than bigger ones. Yet another name for this species is "Himalayan black bear," reminding us where many of them live.

Even in the mountains, pressures from man are constantly growing. Forests are chopped into small blocks, none of them big enough to support a family of bears. In several of the countries where black bears live, governments with good intentions but little money to spare set up forest reserves, trying to provide areas where the bears can live in peace. But the same areas of forest are usually hunting grounds for the local villagers, who rely on them for food, timber to build their houses, and fuel.

The people are usually farmers, and very poor. Told that they can no longer hunt or cut timber without breaking the law, they are unlikely to join in protecting the bears that have taken away part of their living. When times are hard, they hunt them anyway. A plump black bear provides a lot of meat and fat for hungry villagers, and dealers who buy animals for zoos and circuses pay a good price for healthy young cubs.

Fierce bears?

MIGRANT BEARS

In winter, these bears live mostly in forests below about 4,500 ft. (1,400 m), patrolling extensive ranges in search of food. Pregnant females find dens to sleep in, producing their two or three cubs in January or February. During the hardest weeks of winter, males too sometimes disappear into dens. In late March or April, when the weather improves, the bears leave the lower forests and climb towards the heights, mothers taking their cubs with them. Throughout summer they are often found well above 10,000 ft. (3,000 m), where the air is cooler and there are fewer biting insects to plague them. The first snows of autumn send them back to the warmer regions below.

THE YETI

From time to time visitors to the high Himalayas see a track of footprints in the snow, each more than 1.7 feet (50 cm) long. With five toes spread forwards and a narrow heel, they look like the footprints of an enormous man. In some areas there are legends to match – stories of big, shaggy people standing 6 to 10 feet (2–3 m) tall, who suddenly appear through the mist, then disappear just as quickly. Sometimes they leave tufts of brown fur in the snow. The local name for them is "yeti."

There are similar legends of mysterious "bigfoot" people in other mountain regions of the world, based on similar footprints and sightings. Scientists do not know of people, or even great gorilla-like apes, as big as this. The most likely explanation is – bears. Their footprints are similar to those of a man, though much bigger. Seen standing upright in poor light, the bears themselves look very much like large, shaggy humans. So Himalayan "yetis" are probably Asian black bears, caught by snowstorms high in the mountains, and standing upright when they see strangers approaching.

Asian black bears have a bad reputation. More than most other bears they are blamed for damaging crops, attacking cattle and humans, and breaking into barns and food stores. Does this mean that they are fiercer than other bears?

The people are poor, trying to make the best living they can from a harsh environment. The bears, too, are trying to survive where hundreds of generations of their ancestors lived without trouble. Their main business in life is a constant search for food.

Asian black bear damaging a forest tree by stripping bark

Probably not – it is just that in southeastern Asia they come into conflict with humans more often. This is because human populations in the area are expanding rapidly. Each year more and more people press further and further into "bear country" – the forested regions where, only a few years ago, bears used to be king.

They never have time to learn that farm crops, domestic animals and people are not there for them to eat.

It is not surprising that people and bears, trying to live in the same area, make trouble for each other.

FEEDING

Like most other bears, Asian black bears are omnivorous. Mainly vegetarian, they eat leaves, shoots, roots, berries and fruit. But they are also likely to feed on insects, ground-nesting birds and their eggs, and rodents and other small mammals, including young deer. Along the forest edge they often steal from farmers, taking their crops, honey, cattle and sheep. They are good swimmers, taking fish from lakes and streams.

FACT FILE

Order:	Carnivora (meat-eaters)
Family:	Ursidae (bears)
Latin name:	*Melursus ursinus*
Color:	Black or dark brown, sometimes reddish, with white muzzle, face and chest markings
Length:	5–6.2 ft. (1.5–1.9 m)
Height:	At shoulder 2.5 ft. (75 cm)
Weight:	Up to 240 lbs. (110 kg)
Range:	Nepal, India and Sri Lanka

WHAT IS A SLOTH BEAR?

These are strange, untidy-looking bears, closely related to black bears but smaller and less chunky, with woolly black or dark, reddish-brown coats. The muzzle is usually white or dirty grey, and there is a narrow white chevron (V-shape) on the chest. The fur is thicker in females than males, and thickest of all behind the neck and shoulders. The paws are smaller and more flexible than those of black or brown bears, with long, pale claws that help them to climb. The lips, unusually thick and fleshy, can be curved into a tube - a special device for feeding on termites (see right). An alternative name is 'honey bear'.

Sloth bears have large curved claws, which they use for tree climbing

SLOTH BEARS

Tree-climbing bears of the Indian forests, they feed on leaves, fruit and termites, and often come into conflict with humans at the forest edge.

SLOTH BEARS ARE SHAGGY-COATED bears, closely related to Asian black bears. They look large, almost as bulky as their black bear cousins. But much of their bulk is dense fur. They are neither as fat nor as heavy as typical black or brown bears.

As a result, they are more agile. Though normally slow-moving, they can run quite fast over rough ground, outpacing hunting dogs and people. When alarmed, they climb trees for safety, spiraling easily up the main trunks, using side branches and creepers as their staircase. Despite their size and bulk, they hop and scramble sure-footedly among the branches. When still, they merge with their background, looking just like another part of the tree.

They are most active at night. When all else is quiet, sloth bears can be heard snuffling, sneezing and rustling about on the forest floor. They eat leaves, shoots and fruit, using their large paws like hands to pull food towards themselves, and have a special way of feeding on ants, termites and other colonial insects (see right). During the heat of the day they sleep, often in trees, wedged in a fork, or spread more comfortably on a platform nest of branches and leaves.

Sloth bears live alone, coming together only briefly for mating. Very little is known of their breeding. In the north, most of the cubs are born around June, in the south, at any time of year. Females find a quiet corner of the forest, perhaps a sheltered den between rocks. There they produce a litter of one or two cubs, which they feed for two or three months on their own rich milk. The cubs wander with their mothers for up to three years before setting out on their own.

Fewer sloth bears

HOW LONG DO THEY LIVE?

How long do sloth bears live? We do not know. As in other species, they are most likely to die young, especially during the first few months after they have left their mothers. Those that survive will have learnt more about how to live, and will probably live on a further 10 to 30 years. What do they die of? Again we do not know, except that dozens are shot or trapped every year, either for food or to protect crops that they are damaging.

Sloth bears have always been shy and difficult to count – even to see in the wild – so we do not know how many there have been in the past. For the same reasons, scientists have not been able to study their ways as much as they would have liked. But we do know that sloth bears have disappeared from extensive areas of India and Sri Lanka where they used to live. We know too that, where they still exist, they have become much rarer and harder to find than they were even 50 years ago.

It is not hard to guess the reason. In that time, large areas of their forest have been stripped to provide timber, or cleared altogether for agriculture or towns. Some river valleys and plains, formerly forested, have been dammed and turned into

Performing sloth bear with Indian trainer

lakes, to provide hydroelectric power. Selling timber, growing food and providing electricity were all ways of improving the standard of living of millions of people in Nepal, India and Sri Lanka.

This is a problem that faces governments all over the world – not only in the poorer and wilder countries, but in North America and Europe too. Read more about it on pp. 38–39.

Sloth bear munching leaves and grass

FEEDING

Leaves, buds, shoots and fruit are important in their diet, but sloth bears are also especially fond of ants, termites, bees and other colonial insects. When a bear finds a nest of one of these species, it tears a hole in the side with powerful claws, then inserts its long muzzle, closing its nostrils to keep the insects out. Now the fleshy upper lips curve into a tube, and the bear sucks out the insects, eggs, larvae and honey. To make the suction stronger, some of the front teeth are missing, and the roof of the mouth is hollowed like a tunnel.

WHERE DO WE FIND THEM?

Confined to the foothills of Nepal and the vast, rolling plains of India and Sri Lanka, sloth bears live mainly in lowland forests. They seem to prefer those with low hills and rocky outcrops. The map shows where they used to live. But the spreading of human populations and the destruction of the forests have driven sloth bears from many areas. Today there are not many left, except in national parks and reserves. Those that remain live in the densest, least accessible patches of forest, where they are not at all easy to find.

WHY SLOTH BEARS?

Their name was simply a mistake, made by the museum scientists who first described them. Sloths are smaller, slow-moving animals that spend most of their lives hanging by their claws, often upside-down, from tree branches. The scientists who examined the first skins of these animals to arrive from India read the hunters' descriptions, noted the long claws, and concluded that they must be large sloths, or possibly bears that lived like sloths. But sloth bears are true bears, only distantly related to sloths, and not at all like them in habits.

SUN BEARS

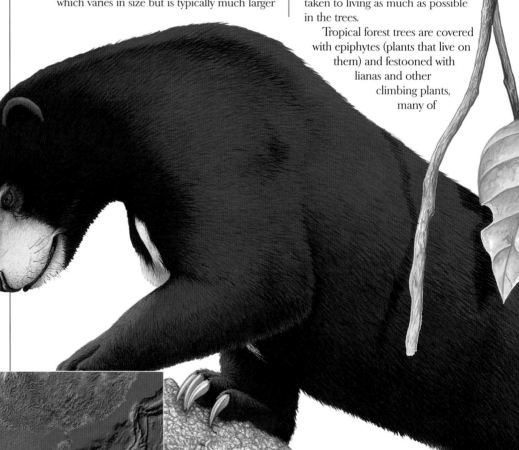

Smallest of the bears, their homes are the trees of tropical rain forests throughout south eastern Asia. There may be only a few thousand left.

FACT FILE

Order:	Carnivora (meat-eaters)
Family:	Ursidae (bears)
Latin name:	*Helarctos malayanus*
Color:	Black or dark brown
Length:	3.3–4.6 ft. (1.0–1.4 m)
Height:	At shoulder 2.3 ft. (70 cm)
Weight:	Up to 140 lbs. (65 kg)
Range:	Assam, Manipur, Burma and Laos south to the Malaya Peninsula, Sumatra, Borneo

WHAT IS A SUN BEAR?

Smallest of all the bears, these are closely related to Asian black bears, but restricted in range to tropical rain forests. They are black or dark brown, with a fawn or yellowish muzzle and chin, and a large pale crescent on the chest that is said to look like the rising sun. Their big front paws, with long, sharp claws, are used for climbing, digging and tearing wood apart. There is no fur between the pads of their paws, perhaps to give them a better grip when they are climbing.

WHERE DO WE FIND THEM?

Sun bears live in the rainforests of south-eastern Asia, from north-eastern India and Burma, through Thailand, Cambodia, Laos and Vietnam to the Malay Peninsula, Sumatra and Borneo. But over this enormous area there may be only a few thousand sun bears. Each bear needs plenty of space, and clearing forests for agriculture and timber has damaged or destroyed much of their original habitat. They sleep during the day and move about at night, so are not easy to see in the wild. At present you are more likely to see them in zoos or game parks than in the forest.

NO BIGGER THAN LARGE DOGS, sun bears are compact, chunky animals with short, smooth fur. The ears are small, the nose is short and the head and body are dark brown or black, with a pale "mask" that includes muzzle, eyes and chin. Though clearly members of the black bear family, sun bears are distinguished by the big, pale chest patch, which varies in size but is typically much larger and more prominent than in other species.

Sun bears live in tropical rain forest – the dense green forest that formerly covered so much of southeastern Asia. So thick is the undergrowth, so wet and soggy the ground beneath, that moving at ground level becomes very difficult. Many of the larger animals, including sun bears, have taken to living as much as possible in the trees.

Tropical forest trees are covered with epiphytes (plants that live on them) and festooned with lianas and other climbing plants, many of which produce flowers and fruits. Sun bears feed in these rich natural gardens throughout the year. They nest in the trees, making platforms or tree houses for themselves among the branches. They sleep throughout the intense heat of the day, growing active in the evenings and feeding at night.

Sun bears are not exclusively vegetarian. They also feed on insects, lizards, birds and small mammals that they catch among the tree branches. Ant and bee nests are a special treat. They tear them apart with their claws and scoop out the contents with paws or tongue. Ants bite and bees sting, but sun bears seem not to be bothered by either.

ENEMIES

Fully grown sun bears have few enemies in the forest. They are big enough to defend themselves against any predator they meet in the treetops. On the ground both they and their cubs are more at risk. Cubs especially may be preyed on by tigers and other big cats, and some are eaten by snakes. But their main dangers are from people. Sun bears snuffling along forest trails may be caught and strangled by wire snares (traps) set by local people to catch wild pigs. Occasionally they get into plantations and damage trees. A sun bear may split young palm stems to eat the central pith – and be shot by the plantation manager.

Awkward and bandy-legged on the ground, sun bears are much more at home among tree branches

BREEDING

We know very little of how sun bears breed or rear their young. There are no marked seasons in their forest, so they mate and give birth at any time of the year. Cubs are born in pairs, in dens on the forest floor. At birth each weighs only about 12 ounces (350 g). They are blind, near-naked and helpless, and very dependent on their mothers for at least three to four weeks. Once out of the den, cubs very soon learn to climb. They stay with their mothers for at least a year, possibly longer.

Bears as pets

Because they are small, sun bears have always been popular as pets. Cubs a few weeks old, found in dens on the forest floor, are carried to the market and sold for a good price. They are easily reared on such common household foods as canned milk, bread, meal, honey and vegetables. They quickly attach themselves to whoever feeds and cares for them. They respond to warmth, kindness and petting. They come running when called, they can be house-trained, and they are fun to play with or just to watch.

All this is true while they are young. After a few months, though less than half-grown, they are already very strong. In the wild at this age, young bears test their strength by tearing at tree stumps, gnawing branches and digging into hard, rocky soil with their claws. When house-bound bears test their strength in this way on the furniture and garden, they quickly become unpopular and have to be restrained.

Caged or chained, lonely and no longer free to wander, they become frustrated, cross, ill-tempered and unmanageable. They are expensive to keep, no longer the happy little cubs that everyone loved, and their owners have to get rid of them.

Letting a year-old bear loose in the forest may be one answer, but is not a kindness. In nature the young bear would still be traveling with its mother and

Sun bear in zoo, Thailand

learning every day from her experience. Alone, it is vulnerable to attacks from other bears and predators. If it is not killed, it may well starve to death because it has not learnt what to eat.

The alternative is often to sell former pets to zoos or circuses. This may be even less of a kindness. Some look after their animals well, but others do not, and the happy, friendly little cub may have to endure years of captivity, poor feeding, ill-health and frustration.

An owner pats her half-grown sun bear cub

The true answer to the problem? Do not keep bears as pets, and do whatever you can to stop bears – and other wild animals – being bought and sold like toys.

FACT FILE

Order:	Carnivora (meat-eaters)
Family:	Ursidae (bears)
Latin name:	*Tremarctos ornatus*
Color:	Black or dark brown with white or pale brown markings on face, throat and chest
Length:	4.3–6.6 ft. (1.3–2.0 m)
Height:	At shoulder 2.5 ft. (75 cm)
Weight:	Up to 440 lbs. (200 kg)
Range:	Forested mountains of northwestern South America

WHAT IS A SPECTACLED BEAR?

These are shaggy, brown-to-black bears that live only in the northern forests of the Andes, the chain of mountains forming the western spine of South America. The name comes from their facial markings. In addition to a pale cream or white chin and muzzle, nearly all have pale bands on their faces. In some these form complete rings around the eyes, making them look as though they are wearing large sunglasses.

WHERE DO WE FIND THEM?

Spectacled bears live mainly in the forests of Venezuela, Colombia, Ecuador, Bolivia and Peru. A few have been reported in Panama and Brazil to the north, and in Argentina to the south. There are probably plenty of them, though not so many as there once were, and they are not easy to see in the dense forests. The most likely places to find them are in parks and reserves. Local guides usually know where to look out for them.

SPECTACLED BEARS

Dark tree-living bears of the Andean forests, they lose their homes when the trees are cut for timber.

SPECTACLED BEARS OWE THEIR NAME to the pale lines on their faces. In some, the lines form complete rings around their eyes and look like spectacles. Others have less distinct patterns, but they all have pale facial markings of some kind. South America's only species of bear, they are similar to the black bears of North America, and almost certainly closely related. Their ancestors crossed the Isthmus of Panama many thousands of years ago and spread through the rich forests to the south, eventually forming a new species.

We know little of how spectacled bears live. There are few reports or detailed studies of their way of life. Though some are found in dry lowland scrub among the foothills, they live mostly at heights between 6,000 and 9,000 feet (1,800 and 2,800 m) in dense forests or high grasslands among the mountain peaks. They spend much of their time in the trees, feeding on leaves, shoots and fruit. Sometimes they tear apart stems of palms and other woody plants to eat the soft central pulp. They are reported to be almost entirely vegetarian, and those that live in zoos seem to fare best on vegetable diets. But they probably eat insects and a little meat too.

Spectacled bears roost in rough tree-nests that they make by pulling together leaves and interlocking branches. We know little of their mating and reproduction. Females produce one to three cubs, about the size of small guinea-pigs, in dens on the ground, staying with them constantly for their first few weeks of life. The cubs run and climb with their mothers for at least a year, probably longer.

Though there are probably several thousands of spectacled bears in the whole wide spread of Andean forests, some biologists think of them as an endangered species. This is mainly because so much of their habitat has been destroyed by people.

Mountain forest

Spectacled bears live in an enormous area of forest, an almost continuous spread that covers the mountains of six or more South American countries. The forest is penetrated by steep-sided river valleys and fringed by grasslands, all of which are used by the bears as well as many other kinds of animals.

Though they live in a wide range of habitats from near-desert in the foothills to high mountain scrub 14,000 feet (4,300 m) above sea level, their most favored haunt is dense, damp "cloud forest," a complex kind of forest that grows in many mountainous areas of the Tropics. It forms at the height above sea level where there is usually cloud. This varies from place to place, but often starts about 4,000 feet (1,200 m) above sea level, and extends upwards to about 8,000 feet (2,400 m).

Cool air and constant damp provide good growing conditions, not only for the trees, but for hundreds of different kinds of epiphytes – plants like mosses, lichens, ferns and orchids – that grow on the trunks and branches of the trees. So cloud forests provide a very rich habitat, with plenty of plant life at all levels, and abundant growth throughout the year. Bears that can climb and scramble among the trees find an excellent living in this kind of forest.

Fortunately for the animals, people do not like living in cloud forests. They are too damp and cool, and cereal crops do not grow well there. Though we cut into the cloud forest for timber, hack roads through it and quarry it for minerals, we find less use for it than for the more accessible forests of the lowlands.

Spectacled bear feeding on the forest floor

AN ENDANGERED SPECIES

Biologists are worried that spectacled bears are in danger of dying out. They list them as an "endangered" species. This means they think that more of them are dying than are being replaced by natural reproduction, so there are fewer spectacled bears every year.

Why are so many dying? It could be due to natural changes. Many thousands of species have died out in the past because of changes in climate or food supply, or through natural disasters. But spectacled bears disappear most quickly where they are in closest contact with man – where we cut down their forest or kill too many of them for food. Can we save them? Read more about that on pages 40–41.

FACIAL PATTERNS

Though practically all spectacled bears have streaks of white or creamy fur on their faces, not all have the full "spectacles." Most have a broad pale stripe along either side of the nose, extending down around the lower edge of the cheeks. Usually they have pale lines under the chin as well. Those are the true facial markings of this species. In some individuals the stripes curve upwards over the eyes to form "eyebrows." In some the lines under the cheeks curve upwards at the outer ends. In only a few do the ends of the lines come together to make complete rings around the eyes.

GIANT PANDAS

Neither a panda not a giant, and not quite a bear – but this animal's picture helps to save wildlife all over the world.

FACT FILE

Order:	Carnivora (meat-eaters)
Family:	Ursidae (bears)
Latin name:	*Ailuropoda melanoleuca*
Color:	Black-and-white
Length:	4–5 ft. (1.2–1.5 m)
Height:	At shoulder 2.5 ft. (75 cm)
Weight:	Up to 300 lbs. (140 kg)
Range:	Mountains of south-western China

WHAT IS A GIANT PANDA?

These are shaggy bear-like animals, related (though not very closely) to black and brown bears. They live only in southern China. The body is creamy white, with black legs, a black band across the shoulders, round black ears, black nose and black rings around the eyes. Both muzzle and tail are short. The front paws have small pads, used like thumbs for holding food.

WHERE DO WE FIND THEM?

Though giant pandas once lived in forests throughout southern China and Burma, today they are restricted to China – to the mountains of north and central Szechwan, the southern edge of Kansu Province, and the Chinling Mountains of Shensi Province. They live mainly in dense stands of bamboo, a coarse grass growing to tree height. There are not many of them, and they are hard to spot. You may be fortunate enough to see one in a forest park, but only with a guide who knows just where to find them.

THESE CHUBBY, BEAR-LIKE MAMMALS, though well-known to the Chinese for thousands of years, are some of the last big animals to be described by scientists, and relatively new to the public in Europe and America.

Giant pandas live only in a few areas of cool, damp mountain forest where bamboo is the dominant vegetation. They feed on the new shoots that grow from the clumps of bamboo, but also on stems and leaves of many other kinds of trees and shrubs. Their molars (grinding teeth) are stout and wide, and the fur of their broad face covers a skull with strong bones and massive jaw muscles – a "mill" for shredding and grinding plant material. Mostly vegetarian, they also catch and eat mice, rats, insects and fish.

They live almost entirely on the ground, clambering about in the undergrowth and finding their way into the center of bamboo clumps, where they sit upright to feed. The curious pads on the palms of the front paws act like thumbs, enabling a panda to grasp thin stems and pull them towards itself. Other bears have to do this with their claws, far less efficiently. Young giant pandas climb trees for fun, and to search for fresh shoots. Old ones become too heavy to enjoy the exercise, but climb to get out of the way of predators. Living in dense forest makes pandas difficult to study or count. We do not know how many there were in the past, but their numbers have almost certainly fallen in recent years, and biologists list them as an endangered species. The government of China gives them official protection, but their small, widely scattered populations are difficult to care for and maintain.

A new kind of animal

BREEDING

Giant pandas live alone, coming together only for mating. Most mate in spring (March to May) and produce their cubs in autumn (August or September). Two cubs are born, weighing less than 4 ounces (about 100 g). They are blind for the first six weeks, and begin to move about only after 10 to 11 weeks. Mothers tend them carefully in the den, then take them on patrol in the forests for up to two years.

Giant pandas first came to the notice of European scientists in 1869, when a French missionary, Père Armand David, sent home from China a package of black-and-white furs that he had bought from a farmer. Though an experienced naturalist, he could not identify the skins, but thought he had discovered a new kind of bear.

In Paris the museum scientists disagreed. They matched them instead with the Procyonidae, another group of carnivorous mammals that includes the raccoons and 'cat-bears' or (red) pandas. Though by no means a large animal, it was bigger than other known kinds of panda, and so became the 'giant panda'.

European explorers first saw giant pandas in the wild during an expedition to China in 1913. The first live panda appeared in the United States in 1936, in a Chicago zoo. London Zoo received its first giant panda in 1938. They proved very popular, and more were sent from China, usually as presents from the Chinese government, during the 1950s and 60s.

Attempts to breed from pandas in zoos were seldom successful, so almost all that appeared in public came directly from the forests.

By this time further studies had shown these animals to be closer to bears than to pandas, but it was too late to change their name, so giant pandas they remain.

BAMBOOS

There are many different kinds of bamboo, growing in clumps like tall, coarse grass. The bamboo sticks and poles used by gardeners are dried stems of the same plants. In Eastern countries even bigger ones are used for building. Giant pandas, deer, rats and mice, and several other kinds of animals, browse on these plants, taking the young, green shoots. These look like grass. They are easy to nibble and are rich in nutrients.

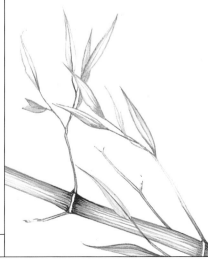

PANDAS AND THE BEAR FAMILY

Scientists disagree strongly on how many kinds of bears exist today, and how many there were in the past. This is because bears are basically very similar, but vary greatly in color and size according to where they live. For example, some say that there is only one kind of brown bear, *Ursus arctos*, which ranges widely over North America, Europe and Asia. They say that Kodiak and grizzly bears are just local variations, with many other varieties, large and small, in other parts of the world. Others say there are dozens of different kinds of brown bears, including several different kinds of grizzly and Kodiak bears, each a different species that should be given a name of its own.

In the same way, black bears can be grouped together as a single species, *Ursus americanus,* or divided into several dozens of local species. Or they can be split into just the two species, American and Asian.

However, most scientists agree that all the brown bears, whether European, Asian or American, are closely related to each other, and also to polar bears. American and Asian black bears, too, form a closely related group, together with sloth bears, sun bears and spectacled bears, which are more distantly related. Cave bears were just one of many species of large bears, perhaps closer to brown bears than to black.

Giant pandas are generally agreed to be a quite different kind of bear. Scientists who first described them thought they were not bears at all. But blood tests have recently shown them to be closer to bears than to any other mammal group, though not especially close to any of the modern species.

BEARS AND HUMANS

*In conflict wherever they meet, bears are bigger
and stronger than humans, but humans carry guns.*

HUNTERS AND HUNTED

Bears came into existence and spread across the world between 20 and 15 million years ago, at a time when there were apes, but before our own species came into existence. Cave bears, brown bears and black bears developed at about the same time as human. These late bears lived mainly in the forests, while humans lived on the plains. Even then bears were probably herbivores, while humans were already spear-throwing hunters.

AGRICULTURE

Hunting by humans destroyed a few bears. Agriculture destroyed many more, by taking away the habitat in which the bears lived. For a long time, right through to the Middle Ages, there was far more forest than farmland in Europe. Bears and people lived side by side. They made up stories and songs about bears, and wove them into their pictures. Then, as human populations expanded, the forests grew smaller and the bears began to disappear.

CHARCOAL BURNING

During the Middle Ages, charcoal, made by heating wood in a pile from which air is excluded, was much needed for burning in stoves, smelting fine steel for swords and armour, and making gunpowder. Woodsmen working in the forests chopped down trees and made great piles of the timber. Charcoal burners covered the piles with damp turf to keep out the air, and set fire to them. After several days' slow burning, the timber had turned into charcoal. Charcoal burning cleared huge areas of European forests, ending when coke (made from coal) was introduced as a substitute.

IN A HISTORY OF ABOUT 20 MILLION YEARS, bears spread across Asia, Europe, North America and the north-western quarter of South America. Their kingdoms were the forests, from which they spread to neighbouring tundra, taiga (forest-grasslands) and high mountain pastures. Adapting and changing as they went, they became highly successful, developing simple but effective skills to cope with their wide range of environments, from hot tropical forests to cold Arctic seas.

Wherever bears lived, they became the dominant species. Though not always the fiercest animals around, they were usually the biggest, with least to fear from the lesser animals that shared their environment. Their dominance went unchallenged until, less than 1 million years ago, a small ape from Africa began to spread across the world.

Humans are animals of open plains rather than forest. Their spreading was bad news for bears. A little larger than the smallest bear, one-tenth the weight of the biggest, he turned out to be a dangerous rival and worse enemy. He is smarter, and demands more land and resources, than any number of bears.

Man began by hunting bears for food. Then, on a much bigger scale, he started to destroy their habitat – the forests where so many bears lived and which many could not live without. Taking

the timber for fuel, housing and furniture, man cleared the ground to graze cattle and grow crops.

This sad history has been repeated wherever man has spread, in Europe, North and South America, India, China, and throughout southeastern Asia. It is still happening in many 'developing' countries – the poorer countries with rapidly expanding populations, which are at present felling their forests to sell timber and create more farmland.

While human populations remain small, there is room for bears and people to live as neighbors. Once human populations start to expand, there is no room for both. Man spreads into the forest, and bears retreat before him. He continues to hunt them. He kills them when they take his cattle, sheep or crops. He kills them for sport, keeps them captive, and puts them on show in circuses and zoos. But the real damage occurs when he cuts down the forest and takes away their home.

PERFORMING BEARS

For centuries, bears have been caught as cubs, reared, and trained to perform tricks such as dancing, pulling carts and riding tricycles. Trainers see something that they do naturally, and persuade them, by rewards and punishments, to do it to order. Bears in the wild, when bored or unsettled, sometimes jig rhythmically up and down. Trainers teach them to jig when they play a drum or blow a trumpet - so the bear seems to be 'dancing'. Bears use their paws to pick up and examine strange objects. Trainers make this seem funny by dressing them in human clothes and making them hold flags, toy guns, rolling pins or other unlikely objects.

Bear-baiting, once a very popular sport, involved putting a bear in a pit with two or three fierce dogs, and allowing them to tear each other to pieces.

Bears and early humans

In primitive societies, a live bear was something to be feared, but killing it brought food, warmth and comfort to a family or village. So a bear was thought to contain a kindly spirit, which was released when the animal allowed itself to be killed. In hunting, it was important to address the bear politely, and kill it only if it was absolutely necessary, so that the spirit would not be offended.

Early hunters, as far apart at North America, Siberia and southern Europe, thought particularly well of bears, featuring them in cave paintings, modeling them in clay, and burying their bones carefully in graves. This was possibly because, when standing upright, a bear looks like a large, strong man – the kind of man that villagers would have wanted for their leader or chief. Families named themselves after bears, adopted them as mascots, made shields from their tough hides, and wore their skins for both warmth and protection.

The Ainu people, who lived in Japan, regarded black bears as sacred animals. They would capture cubs, rear them as honoured members of the family, fatten them carefully, and kill them in special ceremonies. Everyone who ate the meat gained part of the sacred bears' spirit. Many Chinese people today think that particular parts of bears, including meat, bones, grease, bile and fur, are strong medicines that cure illnesses and make people feel young and strong.

EXTINCTION

No species goes on for ever. From time to time species that were once widespread become scarcer and eventually die out, leaving room for others to replace them.

Until recently most extinctions were due to natural causes. For example the dinosaurs and pterodactyls that once dominated the world disappeared because of natural changes in climate and vegetation.

That happened long before humans came on the scene. When species disappear today, the first thing we think is that humans must be responsible. Why? Because the human population has increased very much in the past few decades, and we know that our activities have changed the world a great deal. Sometimes these activities have resulted in the disappearance of species, and we feel guilty for this.

But natural changes like those that killed off the dinosaurs are still happening, and still affecting plants and animals. When a species starts to become scarce,

and we want to protect it and help it to recover, we need first to study it and find out how it lives. Then we need to discover what has altered, and made it become scarce.

Only then can we decide whether it is natural causes or human activities that are responsible. If it is natural causes, there is not usually much that we can do to help. If it is human activities, we may be able to stop or alter whatever we are doing, and then check to see if the species recovers.

Several kinds of bears lived and died out before humans became an important influence in the world. What about those that are at risk today? Are humans responsible? If so, what can we do about it?

BEARS AT RISK

Which species of bears are most endangered?

FROM WHAT WE KNOW AT PRESENT, no whole species of bear is currently in immediate danger of complete extinction. But several have been cut into small populations, or local groups, and some of those may be in serious trouble. For example:

■ Brown bears all over Europe and in many parts of Asia live in small, scattered populations – several of the smallest are in danger of dying out.

■ Several small populations of grizzly bears, which may be species, subspecies or just interesting varieties, are reduced to very small numbers, and may be in danger of dying out.

■ Forest clearance and hunting have quite recently reduced sloth bears of India and Sri Lanka to small, scattered groups, about which we know little – some of these groups are probably too small to survive.

■ Sun bears in southeastern Asia and spectacled bears in South America are likely to suffer the same fate, as human populations take over more and more of their forests.

■ Even giant pandas, world symbol of conservation, are now subdivided into small populations that are quite possibly at risk.

For many populations of bears, we simply do not know enough to judge whether or not they are likely to die out. But where human populations are expanding, the bears are very likely to be in retreat. The best way to protect them is usually to set up reserves and sanctuaries for those remaining, if possible with the help and co-operation of local people, before it is too late.

Bears at risk

Which kinds of bears are currently at risk from hunting or habitat destruction and which are relatively secure?

Eurasian brown bears – Very few are left in western Europe. Local populations in Spain, France and other European countries need careful monitoring. The continuing protection of parks and reserves is also important. In Asia they are probably still plentiful in remote forests. But elsewhere they tend to retreat before expanding human populations. More studies, monitoring and protection are needed.

Siberian brown bears – Though little is known of them, these bears are spread over wide areas of relatively untouched forest.

Though hunted and displaced by industry in some localities, they seem likely to be faring well over most of their extensive range.

Grizzly bears – Some local populations or subspecies are down to low numbers. All need continuing protection in parks and reserves.

Kodiak bears – Most stocks are well cared for. The species seems plentiful and well protected by game laws.

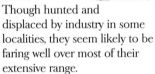

Polar bears – Relatively untouched and unthreatened by man, most stocks are well studied, well protected by international agreement, and appear to be flourishing.

American black bears – Remaining stocks seem to be plentiful, and well protected by game laws.

Asian black bears – These are probably plentiful in some remote forest areas. But many smaller populations are at risk where they come into contact with expanding human populations. They need further study, monitoring and local protection.

Sloth bears – Though there is little information available about them, these may well be the most most seriously threatened of all bears. The population generally appears to have suffered serious decline in recent decades because of human population pressures. They may still be plentiful in small remnant areas of forest, but not elsewhere. There is an urgent need for study, monitoring and protection.

Sun bears – A widespread species, they are probably still plentiful in untouched areas, but are very much at risk from the spread of human activities, notably forest destruction. They are vulnerable to capture for trading, and urgently need further study, monitoring, and local protection in parks and reserves.

Spectacled bears – Though still plentiful in Ecuador and other areas of dense, undamaged forest, they are at risk in other countries, such as Peru, where human activities are spreading into the forests. They urgently need further study, monitoring, and local protection in parks and reserves.

Giant pandas – Though protected by law, several small remnant stocks are almost certainly at risk from local hunting, and both natural and man-made changes in the forests. They need further study, monitoring and local protection.

HOW CAN WE HELP?

You and everyone else can help in these ways:

■ Join a national or international conservation group that aims to protect and conserve wildlife, especially bears. There are several addresses on page 44.
■ Help the group to raise money for research on bears, and to support schemes for their protection.

■ Learn all you can about bears. Read books about them, watch videos and films, and tell all your friends about them. Get as many people as you can to support bear conservation.
■ Remember that where bears live the local people may be very poor. Do not blame them for neglecting or destroying their bears. Support organizations that help bears and people to live alongside each other.

■ If you live in a country that has bears, encourage your government, local government and local community to support wildlife, paying special attention to bears.
■ Visit national parks and reserves where bears live. Ask the park managers, rangers and guides how many bears there are, which species, how they are faring, and where you can see them.

■ Talk to members of local hunting and shooting clubs. Find out what they know about bears, and if they can help you to see them in the wild.

EUROPEAN BROWN BEARS: THE PROBLEM

During the past 500 years, the vast forests that once spread almost continuously across western Europe have been drastically reduced. Much of this clearance has been for farming and the spread of towns and cities. Small remnant patches of forest have been cut by roads, canals and railways, or crossed by fences. As a result, even in the remaining forests, bears and other animals cannot wander freely. It takes a big area of forest to support a brown bear, even more to support a small family.

It is not surprising that, as the forests have declined, so have the bears that depend on them for their living. European brown bears fare best in the still-forested countries of eastern Europe. These countries include Russia east of the Ural Mountains, Belarus, Estonia, Latvia, Lithuania, Moldavia and Ukraine, which together support about 30,000-40,000 brown bears.

Countries of southeastern Europe with extensive forests remaining, such as Bulgaria, the Czech Republic, Romania, Slovakia and former Yugoslavia, have a total population of about 8,000 brown bears between them. However, the northern countries of Sweden, Norway and Finland have only about 1,000. And across the warmer parts of Europe, from Poland in the east to France and the Netherlands in the west, there are probably fewer than 400, in small, widely separated groups.

SAVING THE BEARS

A sad past for bears: can we promise them a better future? This is how European brown bears are being protected.

WHAT IS BEING DONE?

In the forested countries of eastern Europe, the bears will remain safe so long as (1) the forests are protected, (2) hunting is controlled and (3) farmers on the forest edges are either allowed to protect their crops or paid compensation when they suffer damage. Both the government and the people of each country need to be proud of their bears. They have to want to protect them.

Over the rest of Europe, the remaining bears are at risk. And, for the same reasons, so are many other mammals that depend on forest for their living. Protecting them is not a simple matter. There are many different countries involved, all with different laws, and many different people with different attitudes to bears. Some people want to protect them. Others want to destroy them because of the damage they do, especially around farms.

The World Wildlife Fund (WWF) has for many years raised money to help protect wildlife. An important plan called 'Large carnivore initiative for Europe', which started in 1995, sets out to protect wolves, two kinds of lynx, wolverines and other big animals including bears.

The Large Carnivore Initiative

WWF realized that all the big forest animals of Europe are in trouble for the same reason - because so little of their forest home remains. Whatever is good for one species is likely to be good for them all.

They realized, too, that there are many small individual groups of people in all the countries of Europe - including government departments, university researchers, naturalists, clubs and societies - all working in different ways to protect these animals. Some are trying to discover more about how they live. Others are protecting or replanting forest, making laws to control hunting, campaigning against environmental destruction, or simply teaching children and grown-ups about the importance of conservation. They are all doing valuable work, but doing it separately and often without knowing about each other.

The WWF plan works by co-ordinating all these different efforts, bringing them together, giving advice, exchanging ideas, designing management plans and action plans, and collecting money to give wherever it is most needed.

ACTION

Under this plan, WWF has special projects working in the Alps, the Carpathian Mountains, the Balkan countries, the Pyrenees Mountains, Spain and Portugal, and Scandinavia - all areas where small remnant populations of bears are at risk.

In addition, a special action plan for the conservation of bears has been drawn up. Small numbers of bears are being transferred from places where there are plenty of them to areas where they used to live, and will probably live again if protected.

GLOSSARY

Can you identify the species pictured?
(answers below)

adapt	Change in ways that make better or more efficient
aggressive	Likely to attack
Arctic	Area of ice and snow surrounding the North Pole, including northern Alaska, Canada, Greenland, northern Scandinavia and Siberia, the Arctic Ocean and neighboring seas
barren grounds	Cold, dry areas of the Arctic where very little grows
canine (teeth)	Long pointed teeth at the front on either side of the jaws
carnassial (teeth)	Meat-cutting; flat, sharp-edged teeth on either side of the jaw that come together like scissor blades
carnivore	Animal that feeds mainly on the flesh of other animals
conservation	Saving and protecting species, usually by protecting the places where they live
deciduous tree	Tree that sheds its leaves in autumn and grows new ones in spring
density	Number (of animals) in a square mile or kilometer
digestive system	Parts of an animal in which food is broken down and absorbed (mouth, throat, stomach, intestines, etc)
dominant	Most important, able to control others
dormancy	Short sleep, without much fall in body temperature (see hibernation)
epiphyte	Plant that lives on the surface of other plants
forage	Search for food
fossil	Remnant of plant or animal preserved in stone
habitat	Place where a plant or animal lives
herbivore	Animal that feeds mainly on vegetation and plant life
hibernation	Long winter sleep, in which the body temperature comes close to air temperature (see dormancy)
larvae	Young forms of fish, insects, etc
litter	Young family of animals all born at the same time
medieval	Historically, of the Middle Ages, roughly 600 to 1,000 years ago
molar (teeth)	Grinding; broad, flat teeth at the back of the jaws

From top: Kodiak, American black, polar, spectacled

monitoring	Watching carefully to see what progress is being made
nutrients	Chemical components or parts of food that are essential to health
omnivore	Animal that eats both flesh and vegetation
plantation	Group of trees planted by humans, usually to produce a crop, such as coconuts, cocoa or palm oil
polynya	Patch of open water in a large area of sea ice, often kept open constantly by wind or currents
population	Part of a species living in a particular area, sometimes but not always separated geographically from other populations of the same species (see stock)
predator	Fierce animal that hunts, kills and eats other animals
pregnant	Carrying a developing baby inside the body
refuge	Area of forest or other habitat set aside to protect particular animals that live there
scavenge	Eat garbage or old food that has been lying around for some time
spawning	Egg-laying
species	A particular kind of plant or animal
stock	Small group of animals or plants of one species, forming part of a population (see population)
termite	Ant-like insect that lives in colonies of thousands or millions, building large nests for their eggs and larvae
tundra	Kind of vegetation, mainly of low shrubs and small plants, that grows in the Arctic and on mountaintops: the same word is used for the place where this kind of vegetation grows
wilderness	Wild place, almost or completely unaltered by humans

From top: Asian black, Siberian brown, sloth, giant panda

INDEX

USEFUL ADDRESSES

Grizzly Discovery Center
P.O. Box 996
West Yellowstone, MT 59758
(800) 257-2570
info@grizzlydiscoveryctr.com

WWF
1250 Twenty-fourth Street NW
Washington DC
20037-1175
Tel: (202)293-4800
Fax: (202)293-9211